R. Atkinson Fox
William M. Thompson

R. Atkinson Fox & William M. Thompson

Identification & Price Guide
2nd Edition

Patricia L. Gibson

COLLECTORS PRESS, INC.
Portland, Oregon

Photograph of R.A. Fox courtesy Rick & Charlotte Martin

A varying number of images contained herein were originally published by Brown & Bigelow, Inc.

Second Edition, 2000

Printed in the United States of America
10 9 8 7 6 5 4 3 2 1

ISBN 1-888054-37-9 : $19.95
Library of Congress LOC : 99-70639

For a free catalog, write to:

Collectors Press
P.O. Box 230986
Portland OR 97281

Toll free: 1-800-423-1848
or visit our website at: www.collectorspress.com

Contents

R. Atkinson Fox

Fox Pseudonyms

William M. Thompson

Dedicated to my family and friends
and all of the Fox collectors who
have helped me add to my collection.

Acknowledgements

There are many friends, collectors, and family members I would like to thank for their help and support in making this book and for helping me add to my collection over the years.

A special thank you to my son, daughter, and five grandchildren for tolerating my frenzied collection habit.

Thanks go the R.A. Fox Society and its members who continue to offer new information about Fox in their newsletters and at their annual conventions. For information about the society write to Pat Gibson, 38280 Guava Drive, Newark, CA 94560.

Many thanks to my son, Thomas, for the photography of the added works.

I would like to thank all the collectors for their enthusiastic response to the first edition and their requests for a second edition. Finally, a thanks to publisher Richard Perry for agreeing that there is a demand for this second book. Thanks to all of you for making this second edition possible.

R. Atkinson Fox

Introduction

Robert Atkinson Fox was a prolific commercial artist from the early 1900s until about 1930. He was commissioned to illustrate calendars, posters, postcards, picture puzzles, and advertising materials.

Although Fox painted whatever subjects publishers requested – including, in the 1920s, those typical of the Art Deco mode – his strength was naturalism. Although some of his work has beginning collectors confused with that of Maxfield Parrish, Fox was a painter of mainly landscapes, portraits, and rural subjects.

Fox was a professional painter before he turned illustrator. Although little information has been uncovered about his early life, we know that he took up art at an early age. R.A. Fox was born in Toronto, Ontario, Canada, on December 11, 1860, the son of a Presbyterian minister. He left home in his early teens – apparently to further his study of art. For four years he studied art with John Wesley Bridgman, a portrait painter and member of the Ontario Society of Artists.

From about age seventeen to twenty-five, Fox earned his living as a portrait artist. He painted the portraits of such notables as President Grover Cleveland, President Benjamin Harrison, Sir John MacDonald, along with most of the presidents of his time. Fox's paintings were exhibited at both the Ontario Society of Artists and the Royal Canadian Academy of Arts. At some point in his twenties he studied art and traveled in Europe. Some speculate that the Barbizon School of Painters in Paris influenced him. Like them, Fox used soft and light colors to create a mood of gentle, natural beauty.

In the late 1880s, Fox moved to New York City. In the 1890s, his paintings were auctioned in New York and Boston, exhibited with the Art Club of Philadelphia, and the New York Academy.

At the turn of the century, Fox moved to Philadelphia, where he married a concert pianist. Nothing more is known about his first wife except that she died in 1901. Fox did not discuss any details of this period of his personal life with his later family and friends.

In 1903 Fox married Ann Marie Gaffney of Salem, Massachusetts. Anna was then twenty-five years of age and Fox was almost forty-three. Numerous births and frequent moves marked their early years. Between 1904 and 1920, Anna gave birth to eight children. As the Fox family grew, so did his fortune as he expanded his clientele among calendar, printing, and picture-frame companies. During this time, the family lived in various communities in New Jersey, close to Philadelphia where most of the artist's business was located. They finally settled on a farm in West Long Branch, New Jersey.

From West Long Branch Fox made frequent trips to Chicago to the home of a major client, the John Baumgarth Company (which was subsequently sold to Brown & Bigelow). After Fox was involved in an automobile accident on one of his business trips, the family decided to move to Chicago to reduce his travel distance.

A tireless worker, Fox painted in his studio every day from memory, sketches, or photographs often completing a painting in a single day. Ironically, he had never been to the West at the time when he painted his Western landscapes.

After his paintings were completed, he would patiently make alterations to them as requested by the publisher. Sometimes, when he was not pleased with his work, he would use a pseudonym on his paintings.

Original Fox oil paintings are not easy to find. One reason could be that late in his career, Fox painted almost exclusively on commission for publication, therefore, he never intended the paintings to last and the companies often destroyed them.

After several years of ill health, Fox died in 1935 of heart disease and arteriosclerosis, which were complicated by bronchitis. His wife, Anna, remained in good health until her death in 1964.

R. Atkinson Fox's prints have been popular among collectors for decades and show no sign of diminishing. "Fox Hunters," as collectors call themselves, hold an annual convention and interest in Fox's works continues to grow.

Market Review

The paintings of R.A. Fox were reproduced for prints to put on various items such as calendars, puzzles, ink blotters, etc. They were also sold to frame companies for pictures.

The sizes indicated in this guide have all been verified, but it is possible that you many encounter a piece that varies from the size that is listed. Further, it is not uncommon to find a Fox that has been cropped or portioned, as Fox collectors like to call it. This is because often times calendar companies would cut an image to fit one of their stock calendar blanks. When reproduced in another size, for instance, one could encounter the entire image. Because of the flexibility of print and framing companies, they were more likely to use the entire image by customizing the frame to the image, as opposed to large calendar companies who commonly customized the image to the frame. The underlying factors in determining value are size, condition, and scarcity. In determining the value of a Fox calendar as opposed to just the image, one can typically add $25 for the calendar.

Damage to a piece in the form of color fading, stains, small and large tears, etc., affects value and will significantly lower the prices listed in this book. However, if the piece is scarce the price may not fluctuate as greatly as it would with the more common pieces. Most collectors believe it is better to collect something hard to find in poor condition that to not own the piece at all.

The original frame adds value to a piece, especially when it is particulary attractive and in good condition. The paper backing behind a print does not affect the value of a Fox, unlike other artists whose works are commonly reproduced even today. Because so few new reproductions exist, it is highly unlikely that what you find framed or unframed is new. Of course, laser copies can be made in virtually any size, but they are easily identified by the shiny paper used, the over exaggerated color, and the poor clarity of the image. Buying from a reputable dealer, however, can almost guarantee that what you buy is original.

Be careful on the Internet. I have seen more reproductions on the Internet than any other place. Many of the Internet sellers of these reproductions claim R.A. Fox collectors have told them it is a Fox, so it must be. This is wrong. If proof does not exist and is not provided, we cannot call it Fox, we call it a Fox "look-a-like."

Following are the only eight (8) Fox reproductions known to have been legitimately reproduced:

1. The Right of Way. 22x17.5 (1986)
2. An Old Fashioned Garden. 22x16 (1988)
3. Sunrise. 20x16 (1989)
4. Giant Steps Falls. 12x9 (1989)
5. Where Brooks Send Up a Cheerful Tune. 20x16 (1989)
6. June Morn. 20x16 (1993)
7. Daughter of the Incas. 10.5x24 (1996)
8. Daughter of the Setting Sun. 12.5x16.5 (1995)

R. Atkinson Fox

Glory of Youth. 20x16, $385. 8x6, $195.

Rose Fair. 13x10, $300. 9.5x7, $235.

Daughter of the American Revolution. 10.5x 9, $295.

Meditation #1. 11x8, $325.

Lenore. 11x8.5, $265.

Untitled. 18x16, $265.

Fascinating. 11x8, $350.

A Fair Guide. 20x16, $345. 10x8, $225.

Water Lilies. 4x6, $250. 3x5, $225.

The Village Belle. 22x28, $425.

Untitled. 26.5x19, $375.

Chrysanthemums. 8x6, $350.

Maud Muller. Postcard, $165.

Untitled. 7.5x2.5, $185.

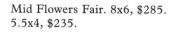

Mid Flowers Fair. 8x6, $285.
5.5x4, $235.

Beauties of the Country. 12x8.5, $265.
Postcard, $95.

A Fair Skipper. 9x4.5, $275.

Pride of the Farm #1. 11.5x9, $345.

The Prize Winner. 11x9, $345.
9x6, $295.

Our Country Cousin. 5.5x4.75, $295.

Untitled. 10x20, $265.

The Best Pie-Maker in Town.
5.5x7.5, $285.

Carefree. 9x11, $350. Fan, $185.

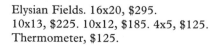

Elysian Fields. 16x20, $295.
10x13, $225. 10x12, $185. 4x5, $125.
Thermometer, $125.

Dawn. 18x30, $350. 10x18, $165.
9x15, $125.

Oriental Dreams. 16x20, $165.
9x12, $125.

Sunset Dreams. 18x30, $350.
10x18, $165. 9x15, $125.

Day Dreams #1. 11x14, $325.
7.5x11, $225. 5x7, $165. Puzzle, $125.

In the Valley of Enchantment.
22x27, $375. 18x22, $325. 9x12, $225.
7x9, $195.

Day Dreams #2. 16x20, $195.
10x12, $125. 4x5, $89.
Greeting Card, $75.

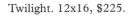

Twilight. 12x16, $225.

Love's Paradise. 18x30, $350.
10x18, $165. 9x15, $125.

My Castle of Dreams. 9x12, $245.
9x14, $225. 7x9, $185.
4.5x7.75, $165. Thermometer, $145.

The Valley of Enchantment #1.
9x12, $225. 6x8, $165. Puzzle, $125.
Card, $60.

Spirit of Youth. 18x30, $350.
10x18, $165. 9x15, $125.

Meditation #2. 8.5x6.5, $250.

The Valley of Enchantment #2.
13x10, $195. 10.5x8.5, $175.
10x5, $95.

Dream Land. 7x6, $155.

Music of the Waters. 20x16, $185.
12x9, $125. 8x6, $95. 5.5x3.75, $95.
Thermometer, $95. Puzzle, $125.
Wood Plaque, $75.

Sunrise #1. 20x16, $225. 16x12, $185.
12x10, $150. 8x6, $110. 5x4, $95.
2.5x4, $75. Metal Box, $110.
Thermometer, $95. Fan, $95.
Ink Blotter, $75. Puzzle, $75.

The Gates of Dreamland.
14x10.5, $325. 8x8.5, $225.

In Old Egyptian Days. 9x7, $295.

Dream Castle. 12x10, $265.
10x8, $185.

Romance Canyon. 18x12, $225.
15x12, $175. 8x6, $125. 3.5x3.75, $75.
Puzzle, $100. Thermometer, $125.
Wood Box, $125. Ink Blotter, $65.

June Morn. 20x13, $285.
18x14.5, $225.

Spirit of the Harvest. 8x6, $295.

A Campfire Girl. 11x9, $265.

Ruth. 11x8.5, $295. Almanac, $145.

Cleopatra. 7x9, $310.

Oriental Beauties. 8x10, $325.
5x7, $275.

The Adventuress. 5x3.75, $225.

In My Garden of Dreams. 23x10, $265.
13x10, $175. 10x8, $135. 8x6, $100.

Deering. 20.5x13.5, $350. 14x11, $295. 13x12, $225.

Jealousy. 16x12, $295. 11.5x8.5, $225.

Faithful and True #2. 8x6, $245.

O.... 15x9, $325.

The Treat. 7x5, $325.

Her Pet. 12x9, $245. 8x6, $185.

Old Pals, 9x7, $275. 6x4, $185.

Ready for a Cantor. 11x8, $275.
Postcard, $95.

Friends #1. 12x9, $295.

Untitled #3. 12x8, $325.

Untitled. 13.25x10.5, $350.

Bluegrass Beauties. 9x7, $285.
Fan, $165.

Untitled #6. 6x4, $285.

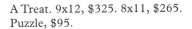

A Treat. 9x12, $325. 8x11, $265.
Puzzle, $95.

Thoroughbreds #1. 12x8, $195.
5x4, $170. Both 1921 Almanac Covers.

Untitled #9. 9x7, $275.

Fooling Him. 6x8, $225.

My Pet. 9.25x6.75, $295.

The Girl of the Golden West #1.
9x6 oval, $345.

In the North Woods. 10x8, $285.
8x6, $225.

Three Friends. 11x8, $325.

The Girl of the Golden West #2.
16x12, $295. 12x10, $225.
Puzzle, $135.

The Blue Ribbon. Magazine, $250.

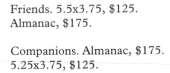

Friends. 5.5x3.75, $125.
Almanac, $175.

Companions. Almanac, $175.
5.25x3.75, $125.

Untitled. 12x8, $265. 11x7, $245.

Untitled. 20x16, $325.

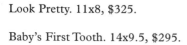

Look Pretty. 11x8, $325.

Baby's First Tooth. 14x9.5, $295.

Life's Greatest Gift. 9x7, $125.
Fan, $75. Sunshine Ad, $135.

An Armful of Joy. 10x8, $125.
8x6, $90.

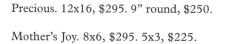

Precious. 12x16, $295. 9" round, $250.

Mother's Joy. 8x6, $295. 5x3, $225.

Mutual Affections. 7x8.5, $225.

Untitled. 9x12, $265.

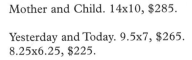

Mother and Child. 14x10, $285.

Yesterday and Today. 9.5x7, $265.
8.25x6.25, $225.

Among the Daisies. 7x10, $295.
3x2.5, $185. Book Cover
"Little Lassies" 1912, $135.

Ring Around Rosy. 5x7, $295.

Untitled. 7.5x2.5, $165.

One Strike. 16.5x9, $325. 9x4.5, $275.

Untitled. 7.5x2.5, $185.

Untitled. 7.5x2.5, $185.

Garden of Contentment #1.
16x12, $195. 10x8, $165. 8.5x6.5, $145.
Fan, $75.

A Safe Companion. 7x10, $295.
6x8, $225.

Warm Friends. 16x11, $225.
14x10, $175. Puzzle, $125.

Untitled #12. 14x11, $375.

A Noble Protector. 20x16, $350.
12x8, $265.

Satisfaction Guaranteed. 8x12, $295.

Bubbles. 8x6, $295.

A Life Saver. 11x8, $295.

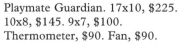

Playmate Guardian. 17x10, $225.
10x8, $145. 9x7, $100.
Thermometer, $90. Fan, $90.

The Barefoot Boy. 16x11, $225.
15x10, $185. Scrapbook Front & Back
Cover, $175. Puzzle, $125.

Please Don't Make Us Go to Bed.
8x6.75, $295.

Faith. 11x8.5, $295.

Me and Rex. 7x10.5, $275.

Going for the Mail. 9x4, $225.

The Fish Story. 7x10.5, $275.

The Old Swimming Hole. 8x5, $185.
5x3, $135.

Prepared. 8.25x11.25, $350.
7.5x10, $300.

You Shan't Go Swimming, So There!
2.75x2, $250.

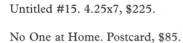

Untitled #15. 4.25x7, $225.

No One at Home. Postcard, $85.

Ready for Anything. 6x8, $250.
Chatter Box Magazine, 1927, $100.
Postcard, $95.

Just Out. Postcard, $85.

Who are You? Postcard, $85.

Too Late. 4.25x12, $250.

Hero of the Alps. 8x6, $265.

Holding an Investigation. Postcard, $85.   Almost. 8x3.25, $275.

Untitled #21. 9.5x7.5, $265.

Thrills Afield. 20x16, $175.
9.5x6.5. $100. 8x6, $85. Puzzle, $95,

Open Season. 6x8, $155.

The Pointer. 12x8.5, $225.

A Reliable Guardian. 16x20, $125.
10x12, $95. 6x8, $75. Puzzle, $95.

On Guard. 11x8, $200. 6x4, $165.

Rover. 5x7.5, $245.

A Trusty Guardian. 7x9. $235.
6x8, $210.

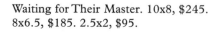

Waiting for Their Master. 10x8, $245.
8x6.5, $185. 2.5x2, $95.

On the Alert. 8x12, $225.

Vigilance. 11.5x10, $175. 11x8, $135.
9x7, $100. 8x6, $90.

The Anxious Mother. 10x4, $245.
8x3.25, $195.

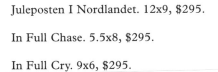

Juleposten I Nordlandet. 12x9, $295.

In Full Chase. 5.5x8, $295.

In Full Cry. 9x6, $295.

Pals. 8x6.5, $225.

An Afternoon Call. 12x10, $195.

Untitled. 21x14, $295. 14x18, $225.

Hunter's Paradise. 16.5x20.5, $165.
12x16, $145. 10x12, $100. 4x5, $75.
Puzzle, $80. Wood Plaque, $65.

At Your Service. 9x6, $250.
Tin Tray, $200.

Ready for All Comers. 19x14, $295.
14x11, $250. 12x10, $195.

Duke. 12x11, $250. 13.5x10.5, $250.

A Gentle Pair. 12.5x8.5, $225.

Good Luck. 7x5, $195.

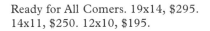

Companion. 10.5x7, $235.

Good Morning. 9.5x7.5, $100.

Fraternally Yours. 20x15, $325.
6x4, $165. Strout Farms Poster, $200.
Strout Farms Metal Tray, $150.
T.V. Tray, $100. Cover, *Strout Farms
Magazine*, $95.

Spick and Span. 12x9, $225.
9x7, $195.

Capital and Labor. 10x6, $235.
3x2, $135.

At the Fountain. 11x8, $245.
9x7, $220.

Tom & Jerry. 9x12, $245.

Two Old Cronies. 9x12, $245.
7x9, $200.

Ready and Willing. 12x8, $235.
10x8, $195. 4x6, $150. 3x3, $95.

Friends #2. 21x16, $325.
5.5x7.5, $195.

Pleading at the Bar. 5.5x8, $195.

Who Said Dinner? 9x12, $245.

Bred in the Purple. 16x20, $265.
8x12, $200. 8x8.5, $165.

Thoroughbreds #2. 12x16, $250.
6x9, $185.

A Neighborly Call. 14x18, $200.
13x16, $185. 11x14, $195.

At the End of a Long Day.
5.5x7.5, $225.

After the Days Work. 6x12, $225.
5x11, $185.

A Legal Holiday. 6.5x14, $245.
5x12, $195.

Ready for the Day's Work. 5.5x11, $255.

Thoroughbreds #3. 6x8, $225.

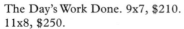

The Day's Work Done. 9x7, $210.
11x8, $250.

Going to the Fire. 13.5x9.5, $295.
9x6.5, $250.

Fording the Stream. 9x5, $265.

Seeking Protection. 10x8, $225.
9x7.5, $185.

Harvesting. 6x8, $225. 5x7, $195.
4.75x5, $150.

Man and Beast Prepare the Land for
the Sowing of the Grain. 17x14, $265.
8.75x6, $185.

The Horse Pasture. 9x12, $200.
4.5x8.5, $185.

Untitled #147. 6x8, $175. 5x7, $160.
Ink Blotter, $95. Puzzle, $85.

Well Shod. 8x8, $245.

Old Rose Bud. 16.5x24.5, on Tin $450.
Derby Day Poster. 16x24, $275.

U.S.A. Quality. 8x10, $225.

A Thoroughbred. Postcard, $95.

Prize Stock. 8x10, $225. 7.5x11, $200.

Upland Pastures. 6x4, $185. 3x2, $135. Puzzles, $95.

The Emperor. 8x6, $250.

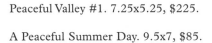

Peaceful Valley #1. 7.25x5.25, $225.

A Peaceful Summer Day. 9.5x7, $85.

A Proud Mother. 10x8, $225. 8x7, $185.

Of Gentle Birth. 6x9, $155.

Pasture Stream. 7x11, $200.
5.5x7.5, $175.

Peaceful Valley #2. 8x12, $235.

Top Notchers. 6x8, $235.

A Land of Milk & Honey. 10x7, $195.
6x4, $135. 3x2, $95.

Untitled #24. 6x4, $195.

The Edge of the Meadow.
10.5x16, $245. Postcard, $85.

In the Pasture Stream. 5x7, $200.

Mid-Summer Afternoon. 8x6, $165.
Puzzle, $75.

A Shady Pool #1. 20x16, $225.
12x9, $195.

When Evening Calls Them Home.
8x6, $200. 9x7, $175.

Untitled #30. 22x14, $265.

Returning From Pasture. 14x10, $225.
13x9, $195. 9x7, $165.

Pax Vobiscum (Peace Be With You).
5.5x7.5, $185.

As the Sun Goes Down. 20x16, $200.
14x11, $165. 12x10, $150. 7x5, $95.
Thermometer, $85.

Peace and Contentment. 11x8, $185.
6x5, $135.

When Evening Shadows Fall #1.
9x7, $145. 7x5, $100.

The Close of Day. 8.25x6.25, $225.

Woodland and Cattle. 16x13, $195.

Untitled. 8x6, $155.

Pride of the Farm #2. 11x9.5, $145.
9.75x7.75, $110. Puzzle, $95.

The Pasture Lane. 15x5, $225.

A Shady Bower. 12x9, $220.

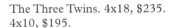

The Three Twins. 4x18, $235.
4x10, $195.

Future Prize Winners. 7.5x10.5, $225.

Four Chums. 7.75x9, $225.

Getting Together. 5x15, $250.

Herefords. 4.25x8.25, $295.

The Watering Place. 5x7, $175.
Postcard, $85. Wood Plaque, $85.

At the Pool. 8x12, $225. 7.5x10, $185.

Thoroughbreds #4. 10x16, $225.

Contentment. 10x7, $225. 7x5, $185.

A Quiet Country Side. 8x10, $245.

A Shady Pool #2. 20x16, $225.
4.5x6.75, $125.

Near Close of Day. 11.5x10, $195.
8x10, $125. Puzzle, $95.

Untitled #33. 16x20, $225.

Peace and Plenty. 8x10, $200.
5x7, $165.

Champions of the West. 8x11, $245.

Browsing. 6x8, $225.

A Summer Day. 7x10.5, $200.
5.5x7.75, $175.

Untitled #36. 10x13, $165. 6x8, $95.

Bonnie J. International Champion.
10.5x14, $225. 3.5x5, $160.

Monarchs of the Prairie. 8x11, $165.
7x10, $145.

Prides of the West. 8x11, $235.

Untitled #39. 6x8.5, $195.

Untitled #45. 6x8, $220.

Untitled #42. 9x12, $225. 6x8, $135.
Postcard, $85.

The Brook. 5x7, $165. 3.5x5.5, $120.
Postcard, $85.

Wending Their Way Homeward.
16x20, $225. 9x12, $175. 6x8, $135.

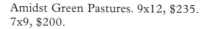

Amidst Green Pastures. 9x12, $235. 7x9, $200.

Short Horns. 9.5x13.5, $225. 5.5x10.5, $180. Puzzle, $95.

In the Meadow Pasture. 9x12, $225.

Scotch Shorthorns. 12x16, $225.

A Bunch of Beauties. 8x10, $245.

Shorthorns Nooning. 11x17.5, $225. 9.5x13.5, $185. 7x10, $160. Puzzle, $85.

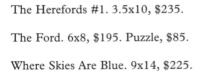

The Herefords #1. 3.5x10, $235.

The Ford. 6x8, $195. Puzzle, $85.

Where Skies Are Blue. 9x14, $225.
8x12, $185.

Untitled #49. 7x10, $285.

Untitled #50. 7x10, $285.

The Herefords #2. 12x16, $225.
8x16, $195. 6x8, $150.

Valley Farm. 9x11, $225. 6x8, $255.

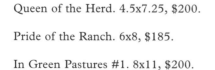

Queen of the Herd. 4.5x7.25, $200.

Pride of the Ranch. 6x8, $185.

In Green Pastures #1. 8x11, $200.

By Winding Stream. 14x20, $225.
9x6, $160. 7x5, $135. Postcard, $95.

Untitled #57. 8.25x11.5, $225.
6.5x9.5, $185.

Prize Winners #1. 22x15, $225.
20x12, $200. 3.5x5, $145.

A Cool Retreat. 8x11, $200.
3.5x7.5, $175.

In Pastures Green. 6x6, $225.

Country Road. 5x7, $200.

Eventide. 6x8, $175.

Untitled. 5x8, $165.

At Sundown. 5x10, $185.

Evening. 7.75x5.5, $195.

An Approaching Storm #1. 8x11, $175.

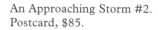

An Approaching Storm #2.
Postcard, $85.

Prize Winners #2. 9.5x9, $195.
7.5x10, $160.

A Blue Ribbon Pair. 12x18, $225.
9x13, $185.

This Good Old Earth. 4x10, $195.

Herefords. 6x9, $135.

Peaceful Valley. 6x3, $145.

American Short Horn. 5x7, $225.   The Wealth of Our Fields. 5x7, $195.

Down on the Farm #1.
4.25x6.25, $220.

Ready For Market. 9x12, $225.

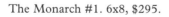

The Monarch #1. 6x8, $295.

Supreme, 9x12, $350.

In the Enemy's Country. 17x25, $385.
10.5x14, $250.

The Challenge. 14x21, $375.
10x14, $325.

A Royal Outlaw. 6x8, $285.
Puzzle, $150.

Look Me in the Eye. 5x3, $185.

Monarch of the North #1.
14.5x10, $375.

A Grizzled Old Grizzly. 5x3, $185.
Ink Blotter, $150.

An Uninvited Guest. 5.5x4, $195.

In the Rockies. 14x12, $225.

High in the Mountains. 20x16, $225. 18x14, $195. 12x10, $160. 8x6, $135.

The Sentry. 16x12, $200. 9x7, $175. Book Cover "In the Jungle," $95.

Eternal Hills. 9x7, $185. 6x4, $165.

The Sentinel. 6x8, $245.

Untitled #60. 12x9, $225. 10x8, $195.

The Silent Rockies. 14x11, $125.
9x7, $85. 7x7, $65. 5x3, $50.
Wood Box Lid, $75.

A Native Son. 7x5.5, $265.

Yosemite Falls. 2.75x2.25, $120.
Ink Blotter, $145.

Mount Hood. 4.25x3.25, $100.
Ink Blotter, $145.

Untitled #63. 15x5, $225.

Their Journey's End. 15x5, $200.
4.5x1.5, $155.

The Feeding Ground. 15x5, $200.
7.5x2.5, $175.

Northward Bound. 16x11, $225.
12.5x8.5, $195. 10x8, $185.

Going South. 5.5x3.5, $155.

Wild Life. 9.5x6, $195.

Startled. 6x12, $195. 7.5x10, $185.

When the Day is Done. 10x6, $125.

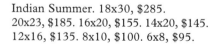

Indian Summer. 18x30, $285.
20x23, $185. 16x20, $155. 14x20, $145.
12x16, $135. 8x10, $100. 6x8, $95.

The Good Shepherd. 12x20, $195.
12x16, $175. 4.75x8, $125.

The Lost Sheep. 6x4, $135. 4x4.75, $95.

In Green Pastures #2. 6x8, $220.

Homeward Bound #1. 8x6, $225.

A Quiet Pool. 6x8, $195. 6x6, $165.

When Shadows Lengthen. 10x8, $165.
7.5x8, $120.

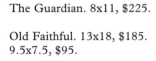

The Guardian. 8x11, $225.

Peaceful Valley #3. 11x8, $185.

Old Faithful. 13x18, $185.
9.5x7.5, $95.

Springs Awakening. 8.5x6, $160.

Watching the Flock. 8x20, $195.

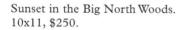

Sunset in the Big North Woods.
10x11, $250.

The Call. 7x10, $250.

The Forest Primeval #1. 8x6, $250.

King of the Silvery Domain.
9.5x7, $150. 7x5, $110. Fan, $95.
Thermometer, $95.

A Danger Signal. 14x9, $225.
10x6, $195. 8x6, $175.

Monarch of the North #2.
15x5, $225. 9x7, $195.

The Patriarch. 5x3, $175.

The Monarch #2. 12x10, $195.
5x3, $155.

Untitled. 9x3, $145.

The Night Call. 9x12, $185.

Battle of the Wild. 19x15, $250.
10x8, $175. 4.5x3.5, $125. Puzzle, $95.

Fury of the Flames. 8x12, $200.

The Morning Call. 8x12, $225.

In the Days of Peace and Plenty.
9x12, $200. 6x8, $175.

A Brother Elk. 12x10, $295. 5x3, $185.

Forest Fire. 10x8, $225.

Evening in the Mountains. 14x10, $185. 11x8, $160.

Nature's Silvery Retreat. 9.5x7, $175.

The Kingdom of the Wild.
6x8.75, $165.

Natures Grandure. 12x20, $155.
6.75x9, $125. Puzzle, $95.

A Sheltering Bower. 20x16, $175.
20x12, $160. 15x11, $135. 5x4, $85.
Thermometer, $85.

Over the Top. 12x9, $200.
11x6.25, $185. 8x6, $145.

Good Morning Deer. 12x10, $125.
5x4, $80.

On Watch. 5.5x3.5, $165.

The Challenge. 3.5x3.5, $100.
Ink Blotter, $145.

Head of the Herd. 5x3, $185.

The Pioneers. 11x19, $275.
10x15, $200.

The Last of the Herd. 10x15, $225.
5x12.5, $200.

King of the Clouds. 5x3, $185.

The Leader. 11x10, $250.

Children of the Forest. 5x3, $185.

Play While You May. 5x3, $185.

Mischief Maker. 5.5x3.5, $185.

Working Overtime. 5x3, $185.
Ink Blotter, $150.

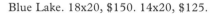

Blue Lake. 18x20, $150. 14x20, $125.

Flower Land. 18x30, $285.

Venetian Garden. 18x30, $325.
12x20, $185. 14x18, $145.

Summer's Glory. 19x32, $375.
18x30, $350.

Dreamland. 14x22, $150. 8x12, $95.

Peace and Sunshine. 21.5x32, $300.
18x30, $285.

Garden of Contentment #2.
12.5x20.5, $165. 10x18, $145.

Nature's Grandeur #1. 14x22, $175.

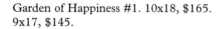

Garden of Happiness #1. 10x18, $165.
9x17, $145.

Sapphire Seas. 14x20, $175.
13x17, $150.

The Magic Pool. 10x16, $125.

Nature's Beauty. 14x28, $225.
14x22, $165. 10x20, $135. Puzzle, $95.

Nature's Treasure(s). 18x30, $300.
14x22, $175.

Garden of Hope. 14x22, $165.
10x16, $125.

Garden of Love. 10x18, $145.
10x12, $125. 9.5x7, $90.
Thermometer, $95. Puzzle, $80.

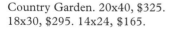

Country Garden. 20x40, $325.
18x30, $295. 14x24, $165.

Promenade. 14x22, $150. 12x20, $135.
8x12, $95.

English Garden. 18x30, $325.
14x20, $145.

Haven of Beauty. 18x30, $325.
10x18, $165.

Land of Dreams. 16x12, $145.
12x6, $100. 10x8, $95. 9x7, $85.
Puzzle, $85. Thermometer, $85.

Love Birds. 16x13, $185. 10x8, $125.
9x7, $95. Puzzle Poster, $125.
Puzzle, $95.

Lover's Bower. 9x7, $165. Fan, $85.

Oh! Rare's the Sunset When Warm
O'er the Lakes. 13x10, $165.
12x9, $150. 10x8, $135.

Untitled #69. 11.5x9, $250.

Majestic Splendor. 30x18. $325.
1/2 Fireplace Screen, $165.

Rose Bower. 16x10, $135.

Dreamy Paradise. 16x12, $175.
14.5x10, $150. 9x7, $100. Puzzle, $95.

Where Memories Stray. 2.75x2.5, $65.
Ink Blotter, $85.

Summer Days. 3.875x3.5, $104.
Ink Blotter, $125.

Fountain of Love. 10x15, $125.

Moonlight and Roses. 14x18, $165.

In a Lovely Garden Where Dreams
Come True. 16x22, $185. 9x12, $145.
7x9, $95. 4x9, $75.

Garden of Romance. 22x14, $150.
10x8, $95.

Garden of Happiness #2. 18x14, $165.
16x12, $145. 9.5x7.5, $125.

Nature's Retreat. 22x14, $185.

Midsummer Magic. 22x14, $150.
12x8, $95.

Garden of Rest. 18x10, $165.

Garden Realm. 20x10, $145.

Blooming Time. 22x16, $225.
18x14, $185. 16x10, $165.

Garden of Nature. 18x10, $165.

Nature's Charms. 22x14, $250.

The Sunny South #1. 16x11, $145.
Fan, $85.

Garden Retreat. 20x10, $145.

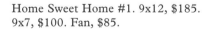

Home Sweet Home #1. 9x12, $185.
9x7, $100. Fan, $85.

Down Memory Lane. 10x6, $185.
9x4, $165.

An Old-Fashioned Garden.
18x30, $325. 16x22, $195. 14x18, $175.

Heart's Desire. 13x27, $275.
14x22, $195. 10x20, $175.

There's No Place Like Home.
15x20, $225. 10x22, $195. 9x12, $165.
7x9, $125. Thermometer, $95.

The Cottage by the Sea. 12x16, $195.
11x14, $165. Puzzle, $95.
Thermometer, $95.

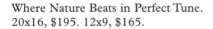

Where Nature Beats in Perfect Tune.
20x16, $195. 12x9, $165.

Wayside House. 30x18, $325.
In Fireplace Screen, $165.

Enchanted Steps. 18x14, $185.
20x12, $175.

It's Only a Cottage / But It's Home.
16x22, $195. 9x12, $165. 7x9, $135.
4x9, $95. Puzzle, $95.

Be It Ever So Humble, There's No
Place Like Home. 16x22, $195.
9x12, $165. 6x8, $135.

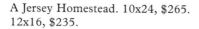

A Jersey Homestead. 10x24, $265.
12x16, $235.

The Old Home. 16x20, $195.
9x12, $145.

Sweet Ol' Spot. 16x20, $195.
15x19, $185. 9x12, $145.

Untitled #72. 20x26, $245.
13.5x16.5, $225.

Just a Place to Call Our Own.
7x9, $175. 6x8, $165.

Memories of Childhood Days.
20x16, $185. 12x9, $135.

When the Day Is Over. 10x8, $185.
9x7, $165.

Home Sweet Home #2. 16x20, $185.
16x22, $185. 9x12, $135.
12.5x12.5, $135. 4x5, $85. Fan, $85.
Ink Blotter, $65.

Cottage by the Sea. 12x10, $225.

Russet Gems. 16x21, $195. 9x12, $145.
4x5, $95. Puzzle, $95.

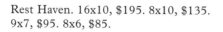

Rest Haven. 16x10, $195. 8x10, $135.
9x7, $95. 8x6, $85.

Down on the Farm #2. 8x11, $175.

Blossom Time. 12x24, $225.
10x20, $185.

A Peaceful Day. 8x10, $225.
6x4, $175.

Peace and Plenty. 16x20, $245.

Down by the Bridge. 9.5x7, $200.
8x6, $175. 5.5x5, $135.
Thermometer, $95.

The Old Mill #1. 10x7.5, $135.
Fan, $95.

Untitled #77. 12x16, $225.
10x14, $185.

The Old Mill #2. 4.5x6, $175.

By the Old Mill Stream. 10x8, $145.
Thermometer, $95. Fan, $85.

Homeward Bound #2. 8x6, $185.
5.5x3.5, $165.

Waiting for the Grist. 6x8, $175.
3.75x4.25, $145.

The Busy Mill. 6x12, $195.

The Mill and the Birches. 10x8, $175.

Summertime at Grandpa's. 8x11, $225.

Untitled #78. 8x20, $250. 8x16, $225.

His First Lesson. 9.5x7.5, $250.

The Old Well. 5x3, $145.

Untitled #84. 4x12, $165. 4x10, $145.

Peace. 12x18, $225. 9x12, $165.
5x8, $130.

Untitled #81. 7x10, $295.

On the Road. 8x6, $285.

Dandelion Time. 10x24, $195.
6x14, $100.

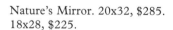

Nature's Mirror. 20x32, $285.
18x28, $225.

Perfect Day. 14x18, $145.

America's Bread Basket. 16x22.5, $225.

After the Harvest #1. 6x7.5, $185.

After the Harvest #2. 7x9, $165.
3.5x8, $100.

After the Havest. 10x8, $165.

Valley of Golden Dreams.
14x11, $185. 12x9, $95. 10x7, $75.
Puzzle, $75.

Rocky Waterway. 16x13, $225.

Untitled #87. 16x10.5, $95.
12x10, $80.

Nature's Sublime Grandeur.
16x20, $145. 9x11.5, $95. 6x8, $75.

Heart of the Hills. 10x8, $100.
9x7, $85.

Bridal Veil Falls – Yosemite.
14x11, $195. 8x6, $135.

The Majesty of Nature. 8x11, $225.

Golden West. 13x15, $195. 10x8, $85.

The Colorful Rockies. 10x8, $95.
Fan, $75.

Nature's Sentinels. 11x8, $185.

Clear Creek Canyon – Colorado.
6x4, $135.

Sunrise #2. 12x8, $155.

The Royal Gorge - Colorado.
9x16, $165. 6x12, $135. 6x4, $95.

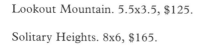

Lookout Mountain. 5.5x3.5, $125.

Solitary Heights. 8x6, $165.

The Approaching Storm. 20x16, $125.
12x9.5, $95.

Moonlight on the Camp #1.
10x8, $165. Puzzle, $95. Fan, $85.

The Winding River. 2x3.5, $75.
Ink Blotter, $95.

Columbia River - Oregon. 14x28, $250.
14x20, $195.

Pure and Healthful. 7.5x10.5, $175.

Canadian Landscape. 14x22, $165.
6x14, $75.

Untitled #90. 16x10, $100.

Untitled #93. 16x10, $100.

The Snowcapped Mountain.
17x14, $165. 10x8, $100. 7.5x5.5, $85.
8.75x2.75, $45. Puzzle, $95. Fan, $85.
Wood Plaque, $65.

The Natural Bridge of Virginia.
6x4, $85. 3.5x2.5, $45.
Ink Blotter, $75. Postcard, $55.

In America's Wonderland.
22x16, $165. 12x10, $100. 10x8, $85.

Untitled #99. 15x28, $225.
12x24, $165.

Untitled #96. 12x22, $200.

Colorado Canyon. 3x2.5, $75.
Ink Blotter, $95.

On the Way to the Mill. 11x6.5, $225.
6x9, $150.

Mountain Vista. 10x7, $185.

Heart of the Selikerts. 11x8, $145.
8x6, $125. 6x4, $100. 3x3, $45.
Ink Blotter, $85.

Giant Steps Falls, B.C. 12x9, $125.
11x8.5, $95.

A Shrine of Nature. 14x11, $185.

Bridal Veil Falls. 3x2.5, $85.
Ink Blotter, $115.

Untitled #102. 10x7.5, $155.

Vernal Falls - Yosemite, California.
6x4, $125. 3x2.5, $85.
Ink Blotter, $115.

Lower Falls - Yellowstone Park.
5.5x5.5, $125.

Great Fall of Yellowstone. 12x8, $125.

Minnehaha Falls. 6x4, $95. 2.5x3, $75.
Ink Blotter, $95.

The Bridal Veil Falls of Yosemite Valley.
12x8, $145. 9x7, $125. 6x3, $95.
Postcard, $85.

Wonders of Nature. 8x10, $195.
Ink Blotter, $95.

Vernal Falls. 11x8, $165.

Yosemite Falls. 5.5x3.5, $125.

Canyon in the Sierras. 9x13, $195.

Crystal Falls. 2.75x3.5, $95.
Ink Blotter, $115.

The Artist Supreme. 14x9, $175.
10x8, $155. 10x6, $135.

Niagara Falls. 6x4, $110. 2.75x2.5, $75.
Ink Blotter, $95.

In the Heart of the Sierra Nevadas.
16x11, $175. 15x10, $155. 9x7, $110.

The Mountain in All Its Glory.
10.5x7, $165.

By a Waterfall. 16x13, $165.
10x7, $95. 7x5, $65. Puzzle, $85.
Wood Box Lid, $85.

Just Before Sunrise. 10x8, $145.
4x3.5, $70. Ink Blotter, $125.

Sentinel of the Ages. 16x11, $135.
11x8.5, $100.

Tourist Mecca. 10x8, $140. 9x7, $115.

Mt. Sir Donald. 3x2.5, $75.
Ink Blotter, $115.

In the Land of the Sky. 12x10, $135.
10x8, $100. 8x6, $95. Fan, $85.

Mt Rainier #1. 16x20, $195.
10x12, $135. 6x8, $100.

Neath Turquoise Skies. 9x7, $100.

Mount Sir Donald – Canada.
16x10.5, $185. 6x4, $100.

In Flanders Field. 10x16, $165.
8x16, $135. 6x12, $100.

Grand Canyon. 5.5x3.5, $125.

The Canyon. 9x7, $185.

Colbourne Buttes - Colorado. 6x4, $145.

Where Giants Wrought. 17x12.5, $185.
6x4, $125.

The Mountain Trail. 21x16, $225.
14x11, $175.

A Glorious Solitude. 8.5x13, $200.
8x11, $185.

Untitled. 9x7, $195.

Majestic Solitude. 16x20, $185.
9x12, $145.

Untitled #106. 8x12, $225.

Sunset Rock (Lookout Mountain).
6x4, $95. 2.75x2.25, $55.
 Ink Blotter, $85. Postcard, $85.

The Gateway to Golden Gorge.
10x8, $95. 10x7, $85. 10x5, $75.
5x3, $55. Fan, $85.

Paradise Bay. 7.5x6.75, $95. 3x2, $55.

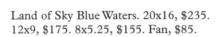

Land of Sky Blue Waters. 20x16, $235.
12x9, $175. 8x5.25, $155. Fan, $85.

A Golden Sunset. 9.5x7, $145.
8x7, $120.

Birch Bordered Waters. 16x10, $185.
10x7, $125.

Where Peace Abides #1. 10x7, $125.
6.25x4.75, $85.

A Mountain Paradise #1. 8x15, $125.

Glorious Vista. 18x30, $250.
16x20, $145. 13x15, $120.

Purple Majesty. 9x14, $195.
8x12, $145. 7x11, $110.

Nature's Grandeur #2. 6x8, $100.

Lake Louise in the Canadian Rockies.
8.25x6.75, $95. 6x4, $85.
3.75x2.5, $55. Ink Blotter, $85.

Untitled. 5x3.75, $135.

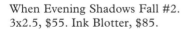

When Evening Shadows Fall #2.
3x2.5, $55. Ink Blotter, $85.

Untitled #108. 6x4, $125.

October Days. 12x9, $135.
9.5x7, $100. 8x6, $85.

Inspiration Inlet. 18x24, $145.
10.5x20.5, $95.

The Home of the West Wind.
16x23, $235. 14x23, $210.
7.25x10, $165. 4.75x6.25, $125.

A Mountain Paradise #2. 16x8.5, $175. 10x7.5, $135.

Lake Louise - Alberta. 11x14, $195.

Mount Rainier #2. 16x10.5, $195. 9x7, $120. 8x6, $100. 6x4, $95.

The Rosy Glow of the Land of Promise. 22x16, $225. 13x10, $145. 10x8, $100. 8x6, $95. Ink Blotter, $85.

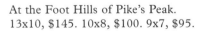

At the Foot Hills of Pike's Peak. 13x10, $145. 10x8, $100. 9x7, $95.

Rocky Mountain Grandeur. 9.5x7, $100.

Among the Snow Capped Peaks of the Rockies. 9x12, $165. 7x9, $130.

Untitled #111. 11x14, $195.

Untitled #114. 13x30, $275. 14x28, $250.

Mountain Lake. 20x40, $350.

Land Where Shamrock Grows.
18x20, $185. 14x20, $165.

Where Peace Abides #2. 9x7, $95.
5.75x3.75, $75.

Twilight Glories. 9.5x8, $120.
Fan, $85.

Glacier Nat'l Park. 5.5x3.5, $125.

Mirror Lake. 5.5x5, $125.

Mount Shasta. 5.5x3.5, $125.

Untitled #117. 11x8, $145.
10x7.5, $110.

Mount Shasta - California. 6x4, $125.
3x2.5, $75.

Head of the Canyon. 10x13, $175.

A Glimpse of the Colorado.
9.5x14, $175.

Guardian of the Valley. 10x15, $120.
9x12, $95. 8x11, $75. 6x8, $65.
6x4.25, $50. Puzzle, $85.

Going to Sun Mountain. 7x5, $85.
6x4, $75. 2.75x2.25, $45.
Ink Blotter, $75.

Grand Canyon – America's Wonderland.
16x22, $225. 9x12, $175. Puzzle, $100.

Mount of the Holy Cross - Colorado.
6x3.5, $100. 3.5x5.5, $75.
Ink Blotter, $85. Postcard, $85.

Mid Mountain Verdure. 8x6, $155.

Untitled #120. 10x7, $135.

A Mountain Lake. 16x20, $175.
9.5x12, $135.

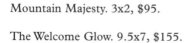

Mountain Majesty. 3x2, $95.

The Welcome Glow. 9.5x7, $155.

Mt. Rainier Glowing in Rosy
Splendor. 13x16, $175. 9x12, $135.
6x9, $100.

Grandeur of Nature. 4x3.5, $95.
Ink Blotter, $125.

Mount Rainier #3. 16x11, $155. 6x4, $95. Postcard, $85.

Untitled #123 (Golden Glow Series). 16x10, $145. 12x9, $95.

Mount Rainier #4. 5.5x3.5, $125.

In God's Wonderland. 13x10, $225. 10x8, $165. 8.75x4.75, $100. 6.5x3.5, $85.

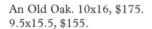

An Old Oak. 10x16, $175.
9.5x15.5, $155.

Mountain Valley. 10x15, $125.

A Fairy-Like Vision: Mount Shasta in
the Sky. 16x22, $250. 8.5x10.5, $195.
4.75x8.5, $155.

Mount Hood. 16x20, $195. 9x12,
$135. 6x8, $85.

Nature's Hidden Places. 11.25x8.75,
$195. 10x8, $175. Fan, $95.

The Witching Hour. 16x10, $185.

The Dells of Wisconsin. 5.5x3.5, $125.

A Song of Evening. 16x10, $125.
Ink Blotter, $85.

Untitled #126. 9.5x15.5, $125.

Sundown on the Marsh. 16x10, $155.

A Silvery Pathway. 9x6, $185.

Morning Mists. 16x10, $155.

Geyser. 20x14, $200. 16x12, $165.
11x8, $145. 11x5, $100.
Travel Magazine Back Cover, $125.

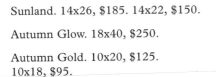

Sunland. 14x26, $185. 14x22, $150.

Autumn Glow. 18x40, $250.

Autumn Gold. 10x20, $125. 10x18, $95.

Pike's Peak From Garden of the Gods. 18x25, $250.

Shower of Daisies. 10x24, $185. 6x14, $75.

Stately Sentinels. 14x22, $155.

Path to the Valley. 16x10, $135.

An Inviting Pathway. 26x17, $185.
20x14, $165. 16x12, $145. 15x10,
$115. 3x2.5, $55. Ink Blotter, $85.

Untitled #129. 18x13.5, $125.
16x10.5, $100.

The Snowcapped Peaks. 11x8, $165.

Mountain Glow. 8x7, $165. 6x5, $125.

The Mediterranean Coast. 22x14, $195.

The Magic Forest. 16x12, $175.
12x9, $135. 9x7, $100.

Shady Glen. 2.75x3.5, $95.
Ink Blotter, $125.

Perspective. 18x14, $135. 16x10, $125.
3x2.5, $55. Ink Blotter, $85.

The Good Luck Line. 10x16, $125.

Untitled. 7x9, $185.

End of the Trail. 4x3.5, $70.
Ink Blotter, $85.

Untitled #132. 16x10, $125.

The Path to Home. 6x8, $175.

Untitled #135. 10x8, $165. 9x7, $135.

Ruins of Ticonderoga. 9x11, $185.
6x7.5, $155.

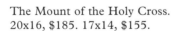

The Mount of the Holy Cross.
20x16, $185. 17x14, $155.

Oaks by the Roadside. 10.5x16, $125.

The Glories of Autumn. 10x24, $225.
10x22, $195.

Spring Beauties. 10x24, $175.
6x14, $65.

Untitled. 7x9.5, $185.

Sunset. 10x13, $95. 8x16, $125.

Where Brooks Send Up a Cheerful
Tune. 20x16, $225. 14x11, $165.
12x9, $135. 8x16, $135.

Popocatapel - Mexico. 6x4, $100.

The Road of Poplars. 8x16, $95.

After the Storm. 11x16, $95.
9.5x15, $85. 10x12, $75.

A Rustic Bridge. 10x16, $125.
Tray, $100.

Pike's Peak - Colorado. 6x4, $100.

The Mystic Hour. 11x8.5, $195.
7x5, $155.

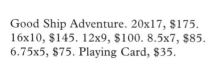

Good Ship Adventure. 20x17, $175.
16x10, $145. 12x9, $100. 8.5x7, $85.
6.75x5, $75. Playing Card, $35.

The Port of Heart's Desire.
15x11, $165. 12x9, $100. Puzzle, $95.
Fan, $85.

Spirit of Adventure. 9.5x7, $145.
9x4, $95.

Vikings Bold. 4x7.5, $175.
6.75x4.5, $100. Cover to Tablet, $85.

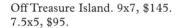

Off Treasure Island. 9x7, $145.
7.5x5, $95.

Clipper Ship. 14x18, $95.

River of Romance. 8x14, $155.
5x7, $100. Puzzle, $85.

Old Ironsides. 9.5x13, $165.
8x12, $135.

Sunset in Normandy. 16x21, $325.

The Treasure Fleet. 9x12, $145.
8x11, $100. 6x10, $95. 4.25x7.75, $85.

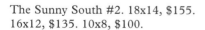

The Sunny South #2. 18x14, $155.
16x12, $135. 10x8, $100.

In New York Bay. 6x4, $135.
Ink Blotter, $95.

The Stairway. 10x7.5, $175.
6.5x4.75, $155. Fan, $95.

The Heights of Quebec. 10x5, $155.
6x4, $135. Ink Blotter, $85.

Kap Nome, Alaska. 8x11, $185.
3.75x5.75, $135.

Palisades of the Hudson.
5.5x3.5, $125.

Pinnacles of Palisades. 2.75x2.75, $125.

Cool & Refreshing. 7.5x10.5, $185.

Sunrise, Coast of Maine. 7.5x10.5, $185.
4x6, $135.

On the Alert. 14x10, $295.

Moonbeam Enchantment. 9x7, $155.
8x6, $145.

Where Dreams Come True.
16x10, $185. 9x7, $145.

Thousand Islands. 5.5x3.5, $125.

A New England Coast. 3x2.5, $135.

The Golden Gate at San Francisco. 7x5, $135. 6x4, $100. 3.5x2.5, $55. Ink Blotter, $85.

The Three Pals. 9x12, $195. 7x9, $145.

A Tense Moment. 13x6, $225.
7.75x3.5, $175.

Their Attack Conquered. 9x12, $225.
6x8, $195.

Good Day's Sport. 8x11, $235.

Well Done. 5x8, $195.

With Dog and Gun. 8.5x11, $245.
5x7, $195.

October Sport. 6x8, $195. 5x7, $175.
Puzzle, $125.

Come Along My Beauty. 6x8, $195.
5x3, $165.

Fishermans Luck. 15x5, $225.
12.5x4.75, $195. 7.5x2.5, $175.

A Thrill Before Breakfast. 11x8.5, $245.
8.5x6, $200.

Going After the Big Ones.
7.5x5.5, $200.

Untitled #66. 22x18, $295. 10x8, $175.
Puzzle, $275.

Untitled. 7.5x2.5, $185.

Mount Katadin. 4.25x3.25, $135.

Untitled. 5x7, $165.

His Last Cartridge. 10x8, $185.
8x6, $145.

The Roundup. 10x8, $185. 8x6, $145.

A Thrilling Moment. 6x8, $245.

Untitled. 8x6, $245.

Masterless. 8.5x11, $265.

The Forest Ranger. 12x10, $245.
9x7, $195.

William F. Cody. 13x10, $275.
9x6, $250. 3x2.5, $150.

The Pioneer. 8x4, $225. 7x5, $195.

Oh Susanna - The Covered Wagon.
8x12, $275. 5.5x8, $225.

Through the Mountain Pass.
10x8, $250.

The Right of Way. 22x17.5, $185.
6x8, $185.

The Great Divide. 8.5x12.5, $250.
6x8, $185.

First Tourists Visit Old Faithful.
15x9, $275.

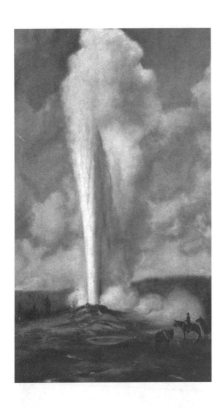

Washburn - Langford Expedition
Discovers Old Faithful. 15x9, $225.

The Covered Wagon Crossing the
Platte River. 9.5x13.5, $250.
8x10, $225. 5x7, $195.

Mount Lefroy. 4x3.5, $175.
Ink Blotter, $95.

The Mountain Lake. 8x6, $185.

Untitled. 7.5x2.5, $175.

Moonlight on the Camp #2.
10x8, $125. Puzzle, $65.

Journey's End - Oregon. 16x22, $275.
10x14, $225.

White Feather. 20x16, $750.
16x12, $550. 15x11, $450.

Daughter of the Setting Sun.
20x16, $450. 16x14, $325.
14x11, $285. Puzzle, $165.

In Meditation Fancy Free.
24.5x19.5, $650. 14x11, $475.
8x6, $245. Fan, $185.

Flower of the Forest. 16x10, $135.
22x18, $155. 9x7, $100.

In Moonlight Blue. 8x6, $175.
7x5, $145.

Daughters of the Incas. 15x11, $450.
9x7, $325.

Untitled #168. 10x7.5, $195.

The Skyline. 9x7, $325.

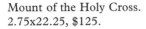

Mount of the Holy Cross.
2.75x22.25, $125.

Good Guide. 12.5x7, $245. 8x6, $195.

Indian Paradise. 12x16, $195.
6.25x8.25, $165. 5x7, $145.
Lid of Box, $145. Plaque, $100.

Edge of Grand Canyon. 8x10, $325.

Among the Rockies. 7x5, $185.

Untitled #171. 8x6, $185.

El Capitan. 4.25x3.25, $165.

The Buffalo Hunt. 8x10, $195.
6x8, $135. Postcard, $85.

Top-Notch Magazine. 10x7, $245.

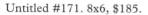

In the Days of `49. 7x11, $325.
6x8, $275.

A Child of Nature. 10x7, $325.

On the Canyon's Edge. 10x8, $245.

Old Faithful by Moonlight. 15x9, $295.

Columbia River, Oregon. 14x28, $265.

In the Foothills. 9.5x8, $225.
6.5x10, $225.

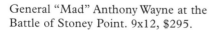

General "Mad" Anthony Wayne at the Battle of Stoney Point. 9x12, $295.

Shouting the Battle Cry of Freedom. 22x16, $325.

The Turn of the Tide - Americans at Chateau Thierry. 8x11, $295.

Tramp, Tramp, Tramp the Boys are Marching. 16.5x12.5, $350.

Surrender of Cornwall at Yorktown. 7x9, $225.

Washington at Valley Forge #1. 9.5x12.5, $295. 8x12, $265.

First Raising of the Stars and Stripes at Valley Forge. 8x12, $195. 8x10, $175.

Washington at Valley Forge #2. 5x3.5, $185. Postcard, $75.

Washington the Soldier. 8.75x 6.75, $165. 4x3, $125. 2x2, $85.

Taking a Trench. 16x20, $295.

General Foch, Pershing and Haig Reviewing Their Victorious Troops. 16x20, $475. 9.25x12.5, $250.

Untitled #141. Candy Box, $325.

Untitled #138. 10x5, $225.
Candy Box, $325.

Supremacy. 16x20, $245.

Untitled #144. 9.5x7.5, $175.
8x6, $145.

Departure of Columbus. 9x12.5, $225.

Andrew Carnegie. 8x5, $175. Ink
Blotter, $135.

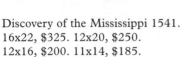

Discovery of the Mississippi 1541.
16x22, $325. 12x20, $250.
12x16, $200. 11x14, $185.

Grover Cleveland. 5x3.5, $175.

Theodore Roosevelt. 2.5x2.5, $135.
Ink Blotter, $155.

Andrew Jackson. 2.5x2.5, $135.
Ink Blotter, $155.

Abraham Lincoln. 2.5x2.5, $135.
Ink Blotter, $155.

The Political Argument. 7.5x10.5, $245.
5x7, $195. Postcard, $85.

Abraham Lincoln. 14x10, $225.
12x10, $200. 11x8, $165. Postcard, $65.

Portrait of George Washington.
22x18, $275. 8x5, $100. Fan, $85.

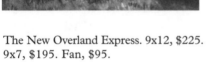

The New Overland Express. 9x12, $225.
9x7, $195. Fan, $95.

An Ambassador of Good Will.
16x22, $265. 10x8, $185. 9x7, $155.
6.5x4.5, $115. Thermometer, $145.

Aces All. 10x8, $285.

The Lone Eagle. 12x16, $250.
6x8, $200.

Out of the Sky He Comes.
7.5x10.5, $275.

Spirit of Discovery. 7.5x10, $275.

The Iron Horse - Driving the Golden
Spike. 18.5x24.5, $350. 6x8, $195.

A Fallen Monarch. 16x20, $225.
10x13, $125.

Between Two Fires. 7x10, $250.

Chicago, Milwaukee, St. Paul and
Pacific #1. 8x10, $195.

Chicago, Milwaukee, St. Paul and
Pacific #2. 8x10, $195.

Chicago, Milwaukee, St. Paul and
Pacific #3. 8x10, $195.

Chicago, Milwaukee, St. Paul and
Pacific #4. 8x10, $195.

Chicago, Milwaukee, St. Paul and
Pacific #5. 8x10, $195.

Chicago, Milwaukee, St. Paul and
Pacific #6. 8x10, $195.

Chicago, Milwaukee, St. Paul and
Pacific #7. 8x10, $195.

Chicago, Milwaukee, St. Paul and
Pacific #8. 8x10, $195.

Chicago, Milwaukee, St. Paul and
Pacific #9. 8x10, $195.

Chicago, Milwaukee, St. Paul and
Pacific #10. 8x10, $195.

Chicago, Milwaukee, St. Paul and
Pacific #11. 8x10, $195.

Chicago, Milwaukee, St. Paul and
Pacific #12. 8x10, $195.

Family Picnic. 7x9, $225. Puzzle, $185.

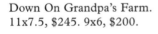

Down On Grandpa's Farm.
11x7.5, $245. 9x6, $200.

Vacation Days at Grandpa's.
10x8, $225.

Mother's Day. 9x7, $250.

Repairing of All Kinds. 13x10, $350.

Untitled #148. 16x20, $250.
13x17, $200.

Gosh! 8x6, $325.

Untitled. 13x6, $285.

News from the Front. 8x5.5, $265.

Faithful and True #1. 7.5x5.5, $295.

Announcing His Promotion.
10x9.5, $225.

Poppies. 18x30, $325. 15x20, $185. 12x20, $135.

Flight to Egypt. 14x10, $265. 8.5x7, $200. Fan, $155.

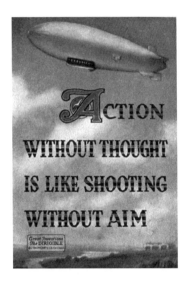

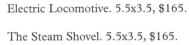

Electric Locomotive. 5.5x3.5, $165.

The Steam Shovel. 5.5x3.5, $165.

The Dirigible. 5.5x3.5, $165.

The Electric Light. 5.5x3.5, $165.

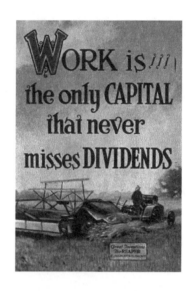

Bessemer Steel. 5.5x3.5, $165.

The Radio. 5.5x3.5, $165.

The Reaper. 5.5x3.5, $165.

The Cotton Gin. 5.5x3.5, $165.

The Telephone. 5.5x3.5, $165.

The Telescope. 5.5x3.5, $165.

Block Signals. 5.5x3.5, $165.

Printing. 5.5x3.5, $165.

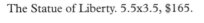

The Statue of Liberty. 5.5x3.5, $165.

The Railroad. 5.5x3.5, $165.

The Skyscraper. 5.5x3.5, $165.

The Brooklyn Bridge. 5.5x3.5, $165.

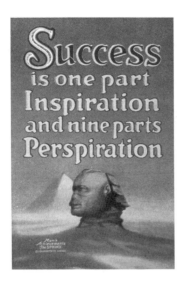

The Sphinx. 5.5x3.5, $165.

The Aeroplane. 5.5x3.5, $165.

The Panama Canal. 5.5x3.5, $165.

Literature. 5.5x3.5, $165.

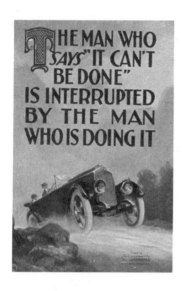

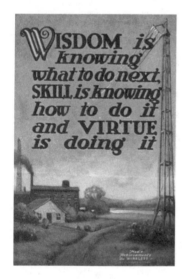

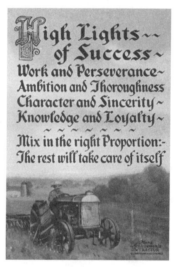

The Automobile. 5.5x3.5, $165.

The Wireless. 5.5x3.5, $165.

The Ocean Greyhound. 5.5x3.5, $165.

The Tractor. 5.5x3.5, $165.

Fox Pseudonyms

Fox pseudonyms are sought after just as avidly as pieces signed by his legal name. Some speculate that he used other names because he was not happy with his work or the publisher wanted to use different artist names for a collection of Fox's work

Decedents of the Fox family and painting records from print and calendar companies have verified that the other signatures in this chapter are that of R.A. Fox's. There are other artworks that resemble the style in which Fox painted and are signed by other names than what is listed below. Those names however, have not been proven and would only confuse the matter further by including them here.

Following is the list of proven Fox pseudonyms as found in this chapter:

1. J.H. Banks
2. G. Blanchard Carr or B. Carr
3. John Colvin or J. Colvin
4. Arthur DeForest or DeForest
5. Dupre
6. Elmer Lewis
7. Musson; H. Musson; Ed. Musson or Edw. Musson
8. George W. Turner
9. Wainright; Charles Wainright; Chs. Wainright; C. N. Wainwright; C. Wainright; C. Wain; F. Wainright; Thos. Wainright or Wainwright
10. George White; Geo. W. White; Geo. White
11. George Wood

Producing the Finest Dairy Products. 10x12, $95.

Cozy Cottage. 14x10, $125.

The Grandeur of Summer.
10x14, $125.

The Garden Home. 14x10, $125.
12x9, $95.

Haven of Splendor. 10x14, $125.
7.5x14, $95.

Watching. 5x7, $100.

Thoroughbreds. 6x8, $165.

Chums. 20x16, $450. 12x8, $225.

On Guard. 7.5x5.5, $225.

Playmates. 16x11, $265. 12x9, $200.

The Guardian. 14.5x10.75, $325.

On Guard. 13x16, $265. 6x4.5, $175.

Faithful. 10x8, $175.

A Faithful Guardian. 9x12, $195.
6x9, $165.

Childhood Days. 9x4, $225.

Untitled #153. 13.5x10.5, $265.

Their First Lesson. 10x11, $225.

Disputed Property. 7x11, $325.

Untitled #150. 8x6, $175.

Happy Days. 8.25x6.25, $250.

Close Friends. 11x9, $165. 10x8, $165.

The Rising Sun. 11x7.75, $175.

Untitled. 9x5.5, $145.

Standback. 11x8, $185.

Untitled. 7x8.5, $185.

Their Great Day. Fan, $225.

Mighty Like a Rose. 10x8, $125.
8x6, $95.

Age of Innocence. 7x5, $145.

Childhood Days. 10x8, $165.

Curly Locks. 9.5x6.5, $125.

Honest An' Truly. 9x8, $235.

Playmates. 10x8, $115. 8x6, $95.

A Bounty From Heaven. 8x6, $135.

Speak Rover. 9x7, $165.

Strictly Confidential. 10x8, $185. 8x6, $140.

A Barrel of Fun. 10x8, $125.

The Children's Hour. 8x6, $145.

Esmeralda. 9x7, $175. 8x6, $165.

Mother's Darling. 8x6, $125.

Meditation. 10x8, $115.

On Treasure Isle. 9x7, $165.

Pride of the Blue Ridge. 9.5x7, $165.

The Adventuress. 13.5x11, $225.
9.5x7, $185.

A Perfect Melody. 9.5x7, $195.

As Twilight Approaches. 10x8, $125.

Mutual Surprise. 10x8, $125.

A Golden Spot. 12x10, $95.
10x71, $85. 6x4, $75.

Aloya of the South Seas. 9.5x7, $285.

The Chieftain's Pride. 16.5x9, $155.
10x8, $120.

In the Land of the Sky Blue Waters.
10x8, $125. 8x6, $95. 4x3.5, $75.

Wanetah. 10x8, $145.

At Peace With the World. 9.5x7, $145. 6.5x4.5, $125.

Dreamy Valley. 10x8, $145.

By the Zuider Zee. 9.5x7, $85. 8x6, $75.

Grandeur of Nature. 10x8, $95. 8x6, $85. 7x6, $65.

Untamed Monarchs. 9x11, $295.

Strength and Security. 15x22, $325.

Safe and Secure. 16x20, $325.
10x12, $295. 9x12, $295.

A Royal Pair. 22x17, $325. 12x8, $250.

Old Ocean Roars - The Jungle
Answers. 12x18, $250. 9x12, $225.
Puzzle, $100.

Master of All He Surveys. 8x10, $285.

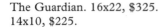

The Guardian. 16x22, $325. 14x10, $225.

Ever Watchful. 9.5x11, $285.

Monarch of All He Surveys. 7.5x5.5, $235. Candy Box, $195.

The Gathering Storm. 10x13.5, $225. 7x9, $225.

Untitled #156. 12x10, $265. 6x4.25, $165.

Discretion is the Better Part of Valor. 10x16, $285. 6x9, $165.

Security. 16x20, $325. 9.5x12, $285.

Safely Guarded. 16x20, $325.
12x12, $225.

On a Trail. 7x9, $225. 6x8, $195.

A Critical Moment. 6x8, $195.

Strength. 10x13, $265.

The Intruders. 6x8, $235.

A Battle Royal. 8x12, $225.

On Rocky Heights. 9x5, $195.

On the Lookout. 14x21, $325.
10x16, $265.

Untitled. 6x8, $135, Postcard, $75.

Washington at the Battle of
Monmouth. 19x16, $225. 12x9, $195.
8x6, $165.

Our First President. 10x8, $195.

Washington at Headquarters.
10x11, $195. 6x8, $150.

The Grip of Winter. 10x3, $135.

The Lure of the Lake. 10x13.5, $175.

Silent Night. 10x13.5, $165.

A Thoroughbred. 10x16, $175.
8x12, $125. 4.75x6.75, $95.

Four of a Kind. 7.75x5.75, $195.

An Interesting Family. 7x10.25, $265.

Untitled #162. 3.5x5.5, $165.

At Eventide. 5.5x7.5, $155.

When the Cows Come Home.
8x6.5, $195.

Under the Maples. 5x7, $185.

The Farm Yard. 7x5, $185.

Off New England Shores. 10x8, $125.   Neath Sunset Skies. 10x7.75, $95.

Silvery Divide. 9.75x7.75, $75.
8x6, $55.

The Flavor of Fall. 10x14, $165.
9.5x12, $125.

Two Medieine River Falls, Montana.
10x8, $65.

The Old Pathway. 13x8, $165.
9.5x6.5, $125.

Sentinels of the Pass. 10x8, $55.

Nature's White Mantle. 9x7, $65.
9x7 All Silver, $55.

At Sundown in the Golden West.
9.5x7, $75. 8x3.5, $55.

Paradise. 12x9, $75. 8x6, $65.

A View Through the Timber. 9x6, $145.

The Babbling Brook. 12x8, $165.

Midsummer. 13x9.5, $165.

Overlooking Emerald Bay. 10x8, $95.

The Campers. 12x6, $145.
16x4.5, $100.

Under the Greenwood Tree.
9.5x12, $165. 6x9, $125.

The Echoing Call. 10x8, $95.

FraLong Fellow Glen. 10.75x6.75, $95.

The Thrill of Freedom. 9x7, $135.

A Garden of Flowers. 17x9.5, $85.
9.5x7, $75. Fan, $50.

100% Pure; Also, Dawn on the Farm.
8.5x10.5, $155.

Untitled #165. 7x11, $125.

The House by the Side of the Road. 16.5x9, $95. 9.5x7, $75.

The Old Fishing Hole. 10x8, $125. 8x6, $100.

Paradise Valley. 12x9, $125. 8x6, $65.

The Favorite. 7x5, $195.

Maid in U.S.A. 8x6, $175.

Being Helpful. 8x6, $250.

Quiet Solitude. 8x14, $155.

Washington & LaFayette at Valley
Forge. 9x7, $185. Fan, $145.

Scenting the Trail. 10x8, $75.

On the Trail. 8x8, $75.

All Set; Also, Hunter's Friend.
9.5x8, $75. 8x6, $55.

At the Foot of Mt. Rainier. 10x8, $75.

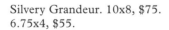

Silvery Grandeur. 10x8, $75.
6.75x4, $55.

Silvery Wonderland. 10x8, $95.

The Sentinel of the Night. 10x12, $85.
6x8, $55.

The Sweetest Flower That Grows.
10x8, $165.

The Girl of the Golden West. 8x6, $95.

By a Falling Crystal Stream. 12x10, $85.

W. M. Thompson
Introduction

Over the years, prints and calendars by William Thompson have been frequently seen at antique shops and shows across the nation. Many know the artist by one of his various signatures - W.M. Thompson, W. Thompson, WMT, or just Thompson. Early works show the signature Will Thompson.

Thompson's increasingly popular works have often been confused with those of R. Atkinson Fox. In fact, many people mistakenly believe that Fox and Thompson are the same person. Thompson's daughter, Dorothy Schwalje, graciously offers the following information about her beloved father:

William McMurray Thompson was born in Philadelphia on May 17, 1893. His artistic talent began to show while he was still in grade school. When he was a young boy, the family moved from Philadelphia to Perth Amboy, New Jersey, where his mother died. When his father remarried life for young Thompson became unhappy for his stepmother was unloving and abusive. He ran away from home, either in 1907 or 1908, and gravitated to the New York City art community.

In New York Thompson worked as an apprentice to William Henry Chandler, beginning as a clean-up boy in Chandler's studio and eventually buying the business. He lived in New York on and off until the onset of World War I and his enlistment in the infantry.

After his return from military service, Thompson married Jean Burnett Drysdale in Perth Amboy on May 24, 1919. The couple resided in that city until 1923, when they and their firstborn moved to a new home in Meterchew, New Jersey. Thompson continued to work in his New York studio, despite chronic eye problems caused by mustard gas during the war.

Thompson's favorite works were done on sketching trips to such places as the lakes and pastures of Vermont, the shorelines of Massachusetts and New Jersey, and the fields, lanes and woods close to home. His last sketches were done on a trip to Lake Louise, Banff National Park, and the Monterey Peninsula. He usually sketched in oils on an 8-by-10 inch canvas board; afterward, in his studio he copied the sketches to larger stretched canvases of various sizes. Many times, pencil and pad were all Thompson used to record a pleasing landscape. In later years he used a camera.

As a commercial artist, Thompson preferred pastels because of their reproductive qualities. Pastels were also quick to make, which enabled him to speedily process orders for greeting card companies and large lithography firms.

During the Great Depression, orders began to dwindle, which forced Thompson to close his New York studio and open one in an upstairs room of his house. But his financial struggles continued; his work came to a virtual standstill. To support his wife and four children, Thompson sought employment with the U.S. government. Once he became acclimated to his new job, he never again worked as a commercial artist. Instead, her served as superintendent of the New Jersey Home for Disabled Veterans until his retirement in 1954. He continued to paint during these years, but only for his own pleasure and that of friends.

Thompson shared with his family the beauty he saw not only in visual art, but also in literature, music, and nature. His daughter remembers him as intelligent, compassionate, gentle, and although not a churchgoer, deeply religious. He adored his children, always encouraging them in their life pursuits, and took enthusiastic pride in their accomplishments. His advice to them was simple: "If you want to paint, first you must draw." And the quote that always brought a smile to his face was "Curved is the line of beauty."

Thompson's marriage was friendly, caring, and comfortable. His wife encouraged and praised him without fail, particularly during the Depression. Because Thompson was terribly modest about the caliber of his work, his wife worked hard to build his confidence and motivation.

In the mid-1950's Thompson's wife died of lung cancer, and shortly thereafter he was diagnosed with Parkinson's disease. The onset of this disease and its symptomatic tremors made it impossible for him to produce the high-quality work he demanded of himself. This was a sad time in his life, as he was unable to artistically express himself in the way he wanted.

In 1966, a fire erupted during the night in the house Thompson shared with his daughter and her family. Thompson's son-in-law, after successfully evacuating his wife and children, lost his life while saving Thompson. The physical and emotional stress of these events worsened Thompson's physical condition, and he died nine months later, on July 29, 1967, in Edison, New Jersey.

During his short but prolific career as a commercial artist, Thompson was widely admired for his renderings of such scenes as Western landscapes, snow-covered countryside, and moonlit campfires. Prints of his pastels, with their subtle blends of colors, are still eagerly sought after today.

Evening. 9.5x7.5, $75.

The Old Home. 9.5x7.5, $75.

Midst Snow and Ice. 14x17, $85.
6x8, $45.

Bright as Day. 16x20, $125.

Autumn Moonlight. 12x16, $85.

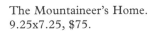

The Mountaineer's Home.
9.25x7.25, $75.

How Dear to My Heart #1. 13x10, $95.

How Dear to My Heart #2.
10x13, $95.

The Dearest Spot on Earth.
9.5x7.5, $85.

Home Is Where the Heart Is. 9x7, $75.

When Shadows Fall. 9.5x7, $75.

Peaceful Valley. 6.75x5, $65.

Untitled #2. 4x3, $55.

Silver Moon. 6x4, $65.

The Day's Long Labor Ends. 8x6, $25.

Breaking Clouds. 6x8, $75.

By the Light of the Silvery Moon.
9.5x7.5, $65.

My Old Kentucky Home. 8.75x7, $75.

Summer Night. 9x11, $95. 6x8, $75.

Moonbeam Reflections. 12x10, $85.

The Moon Bursts Forth in All Its
Glory. 10x12, $95.

Untitled #4. 9.5x7.5, $65.

Eventide. 9.5x7.25, $65. 7.5x5, $50.

In the Gloaming. 10x8, $70. Puzzle, $45.

End of the Trail. 7x5, $55.

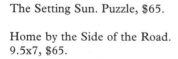

The Setting Sun. Puzzle, $65.

Home by the Side of the Road.
9.5x7, $65.

Autumn's Golden Fleece.
20x 15, $75. 8x6, $45. 4.5x3.5, $25.
3.5x2.5, $20.

Untitled. 12x9, $75.

Memory Lane #1. 9x7, $60.

Memory Lane #2. 10x8, $65.

Untitled #6. 8x10, $70. 6.5x8.5, $60.
Ink Blotter, $45.

The Returning Flock. 14x12, $95.

In the Shock. 8x10, $85.

Untitled #8. 12x9, $65.

Apple Blossom Time. 9.5x6.75, $75.

In Full Blossom. 4x5, $45.

Wayside Scenes. 9.5x7.5, $70.

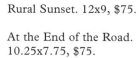

Rural Sunset. 12x9, $75.

At the End of the Road.
10.25x7.75, $75.

Sunset. 9.5x7.5, $75.

Ever Flowing, Ever Turning. 8x6, $65.
Puzzle, $45.

The Abandoned Mill. 7.75x10.25, $85.

Untitled. 12x10, $80.

The Old Water Wheel. 14x10, $85.

Untitled. 6.75x4.75, $50.

Untitled. 10x7.75, $65.

Showering Autumn Leaves. 4x9, $65.

A Frosty Morning. 6x8, $65.

Where the Silver Waters Flow.
7.75x9.75, $75.

Sunset Ridge. 12x9, $75. 8x6, $55.

Untitled #10. 12x10, $75.

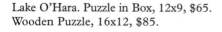

Lake O'Hara. Puzzle in Box, 12x9, $65.
Wooden Puzzle, 16x12, $85.

A Mountain Paradise. 20x16, $85.

Untitled. 18x14, $85.

Untitled #12. 6x8, $55.

Nature's Blue and Gold. 9x12, $75.

Lake Louise. 16x22, $75. 9x12, $55. 6x8, $45.

Untitled. 10.5x7, $65.

Cradled in Mountain Beauty. 15.5x11.5, $75. 12x9, $55. 8x6, $45.

Still Waters. 11.5x4.25, $65.

Spring Time in the Rockies. 9.5x7, $65.
7x5, $45.

The Glory of the West. 9.75x6.75, $65.
7x5, $45.

Moonlight Reflections #1; Also titled,
Moonlight on the Rockies. 9x7, $65.
7x5, $45.

Silvery Moonlight Charms. 9.5x7, $35.

Paradise Valley. 9.5x7.5, $65. 8x6, $55.

Land of the Contented Heart.
10x2.5, $75.

Autumn Brilliance. 8x6, $65. 7x5, $55.

The Gateway of Glory. 9.5x7.5, $65.

Woodland Splendor. 8x10, $75.

Golden Boughs. 10x2.5, $75.

Untitled #16. 12x9, $65. 11x8, $55.
8x6, $45.

Haunt of the Moose. 12x9, $65.

Great Outdoors. 9x11, $75. 7x9, $55.

Flying Low. 6x8, $65.

On the Wing. 12x16, $75. 9x12, $55.
Thermometer, $75.

Untitled #18. 10.5x14.5, $75.

Restless Waters. 9x6.75, $65.

Mountain Glories. 10x8, $65.

Rushing Waters. 9.5x7, $65.

Holy Cross Mountains. 6.75x5, $55.

Sportsmen's Paradise. 9x7, $65.

A Mountain Vista. 7.75x3.5, $65.
12x9, $55.

By a Waterfall. 14.5x9.5, $75.
12x9, $65. 11x7, $55. 10x5, $45.

Twin Falls. 7x5, $55. Puzzle, $45.

God's Handiwork. 13x2.75, $75.

Untitled #26. 9x7, $60. 16x12, $85.

Untitled #28. 16x12, $75. 8x6, $55.

Monarchs of the Golden West.
9x7, $65.

Moonlit Waters. 9x7, $65. 9.5x6.5, $65.

Moonlight Symphony. 13x10, $75.

Gliding Over Boulders. 13x4, $75.

Untitled #24. 16x12, $75.

Untitled #22. 7x5, $55.

The Waterfall. 16x12, $75. 12x9, $55.
Wooden Puzzle, $85. Ink Blotter, $25.

Untitled. 12x9, $65.

Untitled. 11x8, $65.   Untitled. 12x6.5, $60.

Untitled #30. 12x9, $65.

Lake Louise. 16x12, $75. 12x9, $55.
11x7.5, $45.

Natures Majesty. 8.75x7, $55.

Sunset in the Mountains; Also titled,
Golden Waterway. 16x12, $75.
11x8, $65. 9x7, $45.

By a Mountain Stream. 16x11.75, $75.
9x7, $55. 8x6, $45. Thermometer, $65.

Song of the Mountain. 9.25x7, $75.
8x6, $60. Ink Blotter, $35.

Lakeside Camp. 15x11.5, $75.
11x8.5, $55. 9.75x7.75, $45.

Untitled #34. 12x9, $75. 10x8, $65.
7x6, $45.

Silver Moon and Amber Stream.
8x10, $65. 2.75x3.5, $25. Puzzle, $45.

Deep in the Woody Wilderness.
22x16, $85. 12x10, $65.

Pine Camp. 7.75x5.75, $65.

Moonlight at the Fall. 8x6, $65.

Mountain Campfire. 10x7.5, $50.

Moonlight Solitude. 10x7.5, $65.

Untitled #36. 12x16, $75. 9x12, $65.
6x8, $45.

Untitled. 12x9, $80.

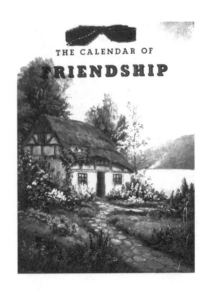

THE CALENDAR OF

FRIENDSHIP

Memories Garden #1. 4x7, $75.

Home & Flowers. 8.25x7, $65.

Untitled #38. 7.5x5.5, $85.

Untitled #40. 12x9, $75.

Untitled #44. 8x6, $65.

Untitled #46. 8x10, $75.

Untitled #42. 8x12, $75.

Memories Garden #2. 9.25x6.75, $75.

Washington's Birth Place - Virginia.
9.75x7.75, $75.

Cottage Neath the Moon. 10x8, $75.

A Breath of Spring. 4x5, $50.

Grandmother's Cottage. 12x16, $75.
9x12, $65. Wooden Puzzle, $85.

Untitled #48. 9x7, $65.

A Spring Morning. 6x8, $65.

A Cozy Cottage. 9x12, $75.

By Placid Lake and Winding Road. 7x5, $65.

Land of Dreams, Pasadena, Cal. 16x20, $125.

Untitled #50. 16x20, $125.

When Winter Rules. 5.75x7.75, $55.
4x6, $45.

Untitled #54. 12x9, $65.

A Wintry Night. 20x14, $75.
16x12, $65. 12x10, $55.

When the Days Grow Shorter.
12x10, $80.

Untitled #52. 8x6, $55.   Untitled. 12x4, $55.

Untitled #56. 12x9, $65.

Silent Winter Night. 6x8, $70.

When Winter Comes Again. 6x8, $55.

Untitled #58. 8x6, $70.

The House By the Side of the Road. 10x8, $75.

Forest in Winter. 8x10.5, $75.

Untitled. 9x12, $85.

Winter Nightfall; Also titled, In
Winter's Ermine Robe. 6x8, $65.

Winter Trail to Home. 10x8, $65.
8x6, $55. 7x5, $40.

Untitled #60. 12x9, $75. 8x6, $65.

A Golden Glow of Welcome.
9.5x7, $60. Thermometer, $55.

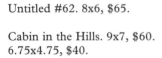

Untitled #62. 8x6, $65.

Silent Night. 9.5x7.5, $75.

Cabin in the Hills. 9x7, $60.
6.75x4.75, $40.

Snow Bound. 10x7.5, $55.

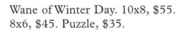

Wane of Winter Day. 10x8, $55.
8x6, $45. Puzzle, $35.

Winter's Crimson Sunset. 16x12, $65.
8x6, $45.

Snow Scene. 9.25x6.75, $65.

Silvery Pathway. 9x7, $65.

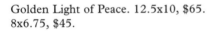

Golden Light of Peace. 12.5x10, $65.
8x6.75, $45.

The Road to Home. 9.25x6.75, $65.

Untitled #64. 5x7, $55.

Winters Silberkleid; Also titled,
Winters Silver and Gold. 13x6.5, $75.
9x7, $65.

Untitled #66. 14x18, $75.

Road to Home; Also titled, When
Winter Comes. 14x10, $75. 12x8, $65.
6.75x5, $45.

Untitled #68. 16x12, $65. 2.5x2, $25.
Ink Blotter, $30.

The Snow is Newly Laid. 4x9.75, $65.

In Winter's Embrace. 9.5x7.5, $65.
7.75x5.75, $55.

Winter Moonlight #1. 9x6.5, $65.

Winter Sunset. 9x7, $65.

Mid Winter Night. 9.5x7.5, $65.

Untitled #72. 6x8, $50.

Untitled #74. 12x16, $75.

Untitled #76. 8x10, $75.

Winter Splendor. 9.75x7.75, $65.

Christmas Eve in the Mountains.
10x8, $75.

A Winter Evening. 12x16, $75.
8x10, $65.

Cozy Cabin. 7.75x10.25, $75.

Where Shelter Awaits. 9.25x6.75, $65.

A Glow of Welcome. 9.5x4.5, $55.

Winter Moonlight #2. 7x5, $55.

Sunset's Mellow Glow. 9.25x6.75, $65.

Untitled #78. 12x9, $65.

The Cheering Welcome Glows.
9.75x7.75, $70.

Twas the Night Before Christmas.
9x12, $75.

Untitled #80. 8x10, $65.

Untitled #82. 10x7.5, $75.

The Light House. 5.75x7.75, $65.

In Full Sail. 6x8, $60.

Homeward Bound. 6x4, $55.

A Moonlight Melody. 10x12, $75.

In the Land of Hearts Desire.
5.75x7.75, $60.

Moonlight Reflections #2. 10x8, $65.

Untitled. 12x9, $95.

Untitled. 8x10, $85.

Moonlight Sail. 10x8, $85.

Where the Sun Sinks Down at the
Close of Day. 14x18, $75. 10x12, $65.

The Land of Loveliness. 15x2.75, $65.

A Tropical Moon. 5.75x7.75, $65.

Rocky Shore. 8x9.75, $65. 6x8, $45.

Midsummer Night. 10.75x8.5, $75.

Sunset Glow. 7x9.5, $65.

Tropical Splendor. 9.75x7.75, $75.

Tropical Moonlight. 10x7.5, $75.
5.5x4, $45.